Without Warning

and Only Sometimes

A story of laughter, love and hope

Kit de Waal

TINDER
PRESS

For

Sheila Doyle and Arthur O'Loughlin,

with love

'We never shall have any more time. We have, and we have always had, all the time there is'

– Arnold Bennett, *How to Live on 24 Hours a Day*

1

I will die.

I will die for wanting Christmas, for the slip of red ribbon from a huge box, for dreaming of the presents inside: Fry's Chocolate Cream, things off the telly, other children's presents. I will die because I want to pull a cracker, because I want to wear a hat. I didn't know about the jokes inside, I didn't know about the little gift inside. I will find out about them when I am seventeen.

I will die for my grinding embarrassment when the teacher halts the school assembly before the worship bit starts, so that me and my sister can walk out.

I will die because, while I sit outside assembly and they sing 'There is a Green Hill Far Away', I sing along but only in my heart. Worst of all, in my heart.

I will die when the earthquakes start. I will be walking to school and the pavement will rumble and hiccup. A crack will start under my feet, small at first, but I will know that the end has come.

I skip the cracked paving stones on my way to school because it can start at any time, the Wrath of God, any moment, without warning. 'Stay on the watch! You do not know the day or the hour.'

Three times every week I am reminded that the world will end and I will die. Only Kim wants to go and worship. She's older than me and seems to understand better than the rest of us. She has let it into her heart and it has made her good. We each have a Bible and our *Awake!* or *The Watchtower* magazine.

The Kingdom Hall of Jehovah's Witnesses, an old building halfway up a narrow road in a shabby part of south Birmingham, is cold and damp. It begins with a song.

> Jehovah made a promise because
>   he loves us so
> To cleanse the earth of evil, of pain,
>   of sin, of woe
> He'll usher in a pure clean world for
>   all of us who sigh
> A Paradise, a Paradise, where we will
>   never die!

Our mother croons and raises her chin to the Lord. This is the highlight of her week. She closes her eyes and lingers on the last note. Too loud, too long. Someone turns round and looks. I crumple inside.

Two hours on a Thursday, two hours on a Sunday, we repeat the trip to the Kingdom Hall. And then every Tuesday there's one dreaded and intimate hour of House Meeting in the cramped, airless front room of a faithful family.

I sit and fidget and cough and turn the pages of the Bible to and fro, to and fro, until I am stretched to the edge of my patience. I am missing *Top of the Pops*. I am missing *Monty Python*. I won't know what to say at school when everyone else talks about the dead parrot.

I live with the dread that one day when my young muscles rebel, can take no more stillness, I will stand and strip naked and burst out of my skin.

I won't burst out of my skin until I am twenty-one.

2

Black Nana's favourite place is sitting on a rocking chair with Tracey on her long lap. She lets the baby play with her beads, and bounces her gently up and down.

Mom goes to work really early, so Black Nana has to get us up for school in the morning.

Black Nana carries Tracey downstairs even though she's nearly three, and me and Kim have to follow her down and into the back room by the kitchen.

Black Nana puts a dish of porridge on the table for each of us and we watch with desperate eyes as she sprinkles a pinch of sugar on the skin. I scoop all the sugar off in one go and eat it in one beautiful, sweet moment of joy. Then comes the misery of finishing it all up.

I have to concentrate on swallowing and not thinking, not even tasting it until it's all gone. I show Black Nana my dish.

'Good,' is her answer as she weaves my plaits extra tight to stop the wispy bits escaping. My whole forehead stretches and stings, but I am silent.

Black Nana walks us to the front door and then stands by the gate to watch us cross the busy road. Tracey is in the crook of her arm sucking her thumb. Black Nana is tall, tall like my father. She could watch us until we disappeared if she wanted to, but when we turn round she's gone.

My teacher at Springfield Junior and Infant School is Mrs Hunter. I do as I am told. Every single child is bigger than me, and I have the feeling that I will never catch them up.

I have a desk all to myself next to a girl with a funny name, Cressida. Cressida has the widest smile I've ever seen and she has freckles. We both get a small bottle of milk with a white paper straw, and have to line up to get a biscuit from Mrs Hunter.

At four o'clock Kim is waiting for me outside school, and Mom is waiting for both of us with Tracey in the big pram. It's feels like a special treat to have Mom come and collect us from school because I know that she is always at work.

Black Nana wears a headtie like a pirate and has a pirate's walk too. One leg is three inches shorter than the other. She sways when she walks, her built-up shoe stamping on the lino so we always know where she is.

I am scared of her, but Kim is not. I think it's

because she's so much older than me, two years nearly, she's a whole six years old.

When Black Nana tells Kim off sometimes, she doesn't say 'Yes, Nana,' like I do. She makes her eyes go narrow and just lets them do all the talking for her.

Black Nana takes Tracey upstairs for her nap and sometimes she forgets to come down so me and Kim have the middle room to ourselves. We drag the broken clothes prop in from the garden and rest it between Nana's rocking chair and the sofa. We're playing horse racing. First Kim neighs and clip-clops over the prop. Then me. Clip-clop, hop and I'm over.

'Quicker!' says Kim and we chase each other over the prop until we're screaming. I'm winning because I'm in the lead and we're pulling each other and pushing, trying to get over the jump the most times. I trip. I fall. My head hits the edge of the prop and I go down crying. Kim kneels down next to me.

'Are you all right?'

But all I do is cry and Kim says 'Shhhhhh!' but I cry loud enough to bring Nana downstairs, to bring her hand across the back of Kim's legs, slapping her three times, hard and quick.

Mom comes back from work really tired and always goes to Kim first. She snuggles her first and cuddles her first because she knows about Black Nana. Then she snuggles me and I try to make it last.

Black Nana holds the baby out for a single minute before bedtime and then Mom has to give her back. Black Nana clasps Tracey to her chest and climbs the stairs to her room. We feel a kind of triumph in her retreat. Mom is back and Black Nana can't tell us off. But we're not sure who is the boss of whom and who is winning the silent war for Tracey.

3

I'm always on the lookout for Dad because, when he comes in, I have to be first. I have to keep my ears open for the exact moment that he opens the front door and then I start running.

'Patches,' he says. He's the only one who calls me Patches because I have patches of pale skin and patches of brown skin on my face. I feel like Patches is our special word.

One day, I hear Dad in the kitchen talking to Mom. I creep to the door and listen. I can hear the clink of his spoon on the Pyrex dish.

'Kim was crying when I got in, Arthur. It's happening all the time these days.'

'Mmm.'

'And do you know what Chrissie's done with the washing?' Somehow Mom makes Black Nana's name sound like she's swearing. 'She's picked out your clothes and her clothes and Tracey's clothes. And left all the rest for me. Mine and Kim's and Mandy's.'

I know he's cutting the soft meat with the edge of the spoon.

'She do it tomorrow,' he says.

'She's supposed to be helping out while I'm at work, Arthur. She's living in my house.'

It's ages before he speaks. The spoon against the dish. The scrape of the chair legs on the lino. The dish in the sink. Then he speaks.

'I say she do it tomorrow. You don't hear?'

That's the voice she never answers. He's the boss of her the way Black Nana is the boss of him. I creep away, back upstairs, silent as a spider.

*

It's my birthday. The last I will have. I am five. A few doors away lives Jane, a big girl, eleven at least, who comes to our house to play with us. She has blond hair that falls all over her face, and she's always shaking it away like a wild horse.

It's a summery day, July bright. Black Nana calls to me from the front door.

'Come, Mandy!' she says. Jane is standing there with a little box wrapped in pink paper and a big pink envelope. She holds them out to me.

'Happy birthday,' she says. 'I can't come round today because we're going on holiday. Bye.'

She skips down the path and I watch her get into one of the only cars on the street with her dad. She waves from the back seat and I wave, too. Then I run inside as fast as I can to open my present. Black Nana stands over me while I carefully pick at the Sellotape on the special wrapping paper. It's just the two of us.

Inside is a golden necklace with a little bird dangling on the chain. It's displayed on a piece of puffy cardboard and wrapped in cellophane.

'Make I show you where I put it,' said Black Nana, snatching it from my hand.

'No! I want it, Nana!' I reach up but it's way too far away.

'Me put it safe,' she says, padding and stamping her way up the stairs.

'But I want it, Nana,' I cry, running after her with my arms outstretched.

Pad, stamp, pad, stamp, good foot, bad foot, good foot, bad foot, up the stairs. She takes me into her forbidden room and puts her hand on the top of the wardrobe. I hear it drop.

'See it there? I look after it.'

She's so tall she can look down at the top of the wardrobe. I cannot. I just can't get up there.

She prods me back down the stairs and outside into the garden.

'Go and play,' she says and I sit on the back step to wait for my mother. I tell her. She does nothing. I try Dad. He does nothing. I ask and ask and ask and then one day Black Nana grabs me by my upper arm. She pulls my face close to hers.

'It gone,' she says. 'I send it home.'

I try to do Kim's trick of telling her I hate her with only my eyes, but they water over and her terrible face begins to blur. I watch her stamp away, good foot, bad foot, and I hate her even more.

Then Black Nana sets fire to Kim.

It's a Saturday and Black Nana is in the kitchen with her back to us.

We sit at the kitchen table colouring in quietly while Nana cooks eggs in a frying pan, spooning boiling lard on them over and over. Kim gets down to watch.

'Move,' Black Nana hisses. 'Move back before you get burn.'

But Kim is fascinated by the slow whitening of the yolk, the rhythmic flick of the spoon in the silver oil, the slight tip of the pan, the blue-and-yellow flames that lick up the side of the cast iron.

'Move!' she says again. But it's too late. All of a sudden Kim's hair is on fire, all the little curls at the top and sides are glowing, sparkling, and bits of hair are floating up to the ceiling. She screams, loud. Black Nana is quick, two slaps of her big hands and the fire is out. She grabs Kim, turns her front and back, claps again. She flicks the blackening, singeing curls, but she's not quick enough. The door flies open and there is Mom with Tracey in her arms.

'What happened?'

The smell tells the tale and Kim buries her head in Mom's skirt.

'You're supposed to be looking after them, Chrissie. All of them.'

My mother's voice is trembling and quiet, not like the voice that's been moaning at Dad for weeks. Chrissie turns her back and flicks the oil over her eggs.

On the day she leaves, Black Nana stands stiff and tall in her uneven shoes, facing my mother in the kitchen. Tracey is cradled in my mother's arms.

'I beg you one more time, Sheila.'

I hear my mother swallow. 'No.'

'Is already two more children you have, Sheila. Two girls. And you not finished having children yet. Give me Tracey.'

Nana's voice takes me by surprise. It's soft, soothing, kind. I shudder.

'I can't do that, Chrissie,' says my mother, holding Tracey tighter, taking a step backwards.

'I love the child. Let me take her. Please.'

My mother says nothing.

When Tracey begins to cry and holds her arms out, Black Nana puts her hand on the door jamb and steadies herself. She looks like she might fall. One final begging look at my mother. Then she turns slowly, awkwardly, and walks down the hallway.

'Go and say goodbye to your grandmother,' Mom says to me. Black Nana turns slightly and, when I'm sure she can see me, I walk upstairs, stamping on each step, good foot, bad foot, all the way to the top.

After eighteen months, there's a telegram. Mom takes it to Dad and, when he opens it, he goes upstairs into the little room where his mother used to sleep.

'Don't make any noise today,' Mom says with her finger on her lips.

Days later, a big photograph arrives in a stiff cardboard envelope. It's Black Nana propped up in her coffin, long and narrow, surrounded by black people, young and old. Unknown relatives, thousands of miles away, showing us how many people turned out for the funeral and what my father got for his money.

I scan the face of every little black girl in the photograph. One of them is wearing my golden necklace under her white funeral clothes.

4

Now that Black Nana has gone and Dean has been born, Mom starts cleaning other people's houses even though ours needs all the cleaning it can get.

One day, a white lady rings the bell. She talks to Mom properly, not like the neighbours who don't like us. She's kind and gives me a very soft pinch on my cheek. She gives Mom a magazine with a drawing of happy people on the front, black people and white people all smiling and standing in a beautiful park.

Mom looks at the beautiful pictures.

'Where is this?' asks Mom. She sounds like a little girl, like someone my age, full of wonder.

'Sheila,' says Stella, holding her hand, 'it's here on earth. Jehovah will bring Armageddon and cleanse the earth of all badness and wickedness, and all the people who are left will make the earth like this, like He always meant it to be.'

When we go to the Kingdom Hall that Sunday, all the Jehovah's Witnesses in the congregation come up to us and say hello. There are white people and black people together, and everyone smiles and says, 'Welcome!' No one looks at my mom like she's no good for having black children and so many of them so close together. Someone gives us a songbook so we can join in, and we sit all together on one row and listen to the man at the front who talks for ages about paradise and how to get there.

Mom gets baptized at the big assembly in London and people start to call her 'Sister'. She learns all the rules and all the things she has to do to actually get to paradise. Play your cards right, keep the rules and you will live for ever.

Of course, it is important to remember that Jehovah made us with free will. For the liars and thieves and people who watch *Top of the Pops* instead of going to the meeting, and for people who accept birthday cards and for people who want to have sex with their boyfriend or girlfriend, there is a terrible death waiting for them. They will die at Armageddon when God brings his righteous judgement on all the evil people in the world with earthquakes and floods and fires and death and destruction.

There isn't long to wait. No. The end will come in 1975 when I am fifteen, in a few years' time, before I leave school, before I grow up. The date has been set by Jehovah and that's the truth.

5

Cressida is now my best friend and I love her. She's funny and smiley and she's eight in April and I'm eight in July so she's older than me and she is very posh. Cressida has her own bedroom and her own toys.

Mr Hargreaves is our teacher, and he was in the war.

He talks about the war like it happened down the road last week and was won by him and his unit, his lads, the boys, us and them, Gerrys everywhere.

'Showed 'em, we did.'

He marches to his desk and writes 'Geography' on the board in a looping, beautiful hand. 'Geo, meaning earth. And what is geography? Hands up. Anyone?'

The creamy light from the high windows falls on my desk. Sometimes when people start talking the sound feels far away and I can think whatever I like.

'DREAMO!'

My heart stops. Mr Hargreaves's face is next to mine.

'DREEAAMMO,' he sings, 'DREEEAAMMMO!' and Pamela Pearson beside me snorts. Pamela Pearson sits at the desk next to mine. Somehow, she has positioned herself between me and Cressida. She has miles of red hair that she wears in a ponytail. Everything about Pamela Pearson is horrible except she's got the best hair in the school.

'Dreeeaammmo,' she whispers.

Mr Hargreaves raps on my desk with his fountain pen. 'What is the earth made of, little Dreamo? Come on now, Dreamo. You were listening, weren't you? What did I say would happen if you kept daydreaming?'

'I'd be in trouble, sir,' I say.

He pulls me out of my chair by my arm. 'And, little Miss Fuzzy Wuzzy, trouble is visited upon you this day.'

He marches me in a soldier's grip to the door of the classroom. He pulls open the door and throws me down on the wooden bench. I have been here before. I will be here again.

For spellings, Mr Hargreaves sits at his desk reading out random words while Pamela Pearson pinches my arm as usual.

'Show me,' she says.

I look at Mr Hargreaves, who is reading the words off a page. I don't answer Pamela Pearson.

'Develop,' says Mr Hargreaves.

I write it down and Pamela Pearson leans over. The pinch is painful.

'Wog,' she whispers. I pretend I can't hear her.

'Blackie!' she hisses.

I look at her. 'Spell it,' I say.

'W.O.G.,' she says.

I smile. 'You can't spell "blackie", can you?'

This time when she pinches me, she turns the skin between her fingers and I gasp. Mr Hargreaves looks up and catches me.

'Finished?' he says. 'No? Then get on with it and stop disturbing Pamela.'

Months of pinching and prodding from Pamela Pearson, weeks of pinches and pokes into my back while I do nothing, has come to this.

'I'm going to get you,' I say to her, and she returns an ugly smile that suits her perfectly.

It's four o'clock and we meet outside in the playground. The word has gone round. There's going to be a scrap. There's a big circle of children all waiting for something to happen. Pamela Pearson is bigger than me and I already know that she's got a massive head start on violence. But, before I can change my mind, Cressida pushes me and someone pushes Pamela Pearson at the same time. We clash together and it starts.

The nasty white girl who lives on the posh street is no match for a bullied black girl who's going to die anyway, who's tired of being the smallest in the class, the hungriest in the class. No match for the girl who is losing her best friend, who has bruises on her arm and bruises on her back.

Pamela Pearson's red hair is her downfall. I pull it down and smack her hard in her face, once, twice, three times, until there is blood. I back off. She starts to cry, stumbling into the crowd as I pick up my satchel and walk home.

My father is leaving for work when I open the front door.

'What happen?' He shoves me into the kitchen. 'Sheilo! Sheilo! Look.'

Only then do I see a strange black lump on my wrist, and feel the scratch across my neck. My mother pulls my cardigan off.

'Who did this?'

She turns me round and examines me back and front.

'Where are they?'

Her face is white and trembling.

'Was it someone at school?'

'It was Pamela Pearson, Mom,' I say and begin to cry.

'The stupid one that keeps copying off you?'

'Yes.'

'When? Where did this happen?'

'Just now in the playground.'

My father comes up close to me. He has to bend from his waist. 'You hit her?'

'Yes, Dad.'

'Who see you?'

'Everybody.'

He stands straight.

'Good,' he says and whistles his way back down the hall, opens the front door and is gone.

6

One day, we come home from school and Dad is in the kitchen.

'Your mother is in hospital,' he says, bending over the cooker, stirring something in a saucepan. 'The baby coming.'

We watch him like he's a magician as he tips in little drops of vanilla essence and stirs, then some nutmeg and more stirring.

'Corn porridge,' he says, like we haven't guessed, like we haven't smelt the grated nutmeg from the front door.

He pours it, thick and golden, on to the waiting plates, where it oozes out right to the rim.

'Careful,' he says as he backs away. 'Eat slow. It hot.' We plunge our spoons in over and over until it's all gone, then run our fingers over the empty plate and lick it clean.

Dad watches us eat with his arms folded.

That's how we eat for the three days that Mom is away.

On the last day when I come in from school

Dad sends us straight upstairs to their bedroom. Mom's in bed.

I notice a new crib next to her and in it is a new, small brown baby. Me, Kim and Tracey crowd around it. Dean is sitting on the bed next to Mom. Kim is first to hold it and then it's my turn.

'Hold your arms like this,' she says and lowers the bundle on to my lap.

'Her name's Karen,' Mom announces and then she quickly takes her away to give to Tracey. When we've all had a hold, we have to go downstairs and sit quietly in the telly room.

Dad forgets to make our porridge that evening. He stays upstairs with the new baby, and the children that they already have are hungry when they go to bed.

Me and Tracey are playing in the big room upstairs. We jump from bed to bed and then on to the little table with four wheels, once on to the floor, up on to the chair, off the chair and on to the bed and round again.

Downstairs, we can hear the radio. Mom always has music on wherever she is and her voice floats upstairs and we join in.

We don't know the rest of the words so we sing it over and over, chasing each other around the bedroom.

'I'm Mr Tambourine Man!'

'No, I'm Mr Tambourine Man!'

And then I land on the table with four wheels and the song changes.

'I can't get no satisfaction! I can't get no satisfaction!'

I'm dancing on the table and there's no room for Tracey so I stay there and raise my arms in the air. She's trying to climb up, but I keep shuffling my feet so there's no room for her. She keeps asking but all I do is sing louder and louder.

'I can't get no, nah, nah, nah, satisfaction!'

When the table starts to tip, I'm not worried. It's done this before and I just land on the bed and bounce off again. But this time when I go down I hit my mouth on the bedstead and everything feels funny. I lie there for a little while because something's happened to my lips and I can't talk. I turn round to Tracey to tell her, but when I open my mouth she screams and runs downstairs.

I run after her and when I get to the bottom of the stairs by the kitchen Mom is standing there with a horrible look on her face. She grabs me and calls for Kim.

'Run over the road to Marge. Tell her to ring an ambulance.'

I keep looking at Mom, wondering why she wants an ambulance, but I can't talk because of the thing in my mouth.

'Don't worry, love,' Mom says, but her face is whiter than usual. She bends down and opens my mouth and puts her finger in and tells me to swallow. When Mom takes her finger out of my mouth, it's covered in blood. Everything is wrong. And now my tongue is beginning to hurt, but every time I go to speak nothing comes out.

'Don't worry, love,' she says again, 'we'll be at the hospital soon,' and then I realize the hospital is for me and I start to cry. I put my arms up for Mom to pick me up, but she's putting Dean at the other end of the pram to the new baby Karen and pushing it out on to the street.

Then Marge is trotting across Springfield Road with her rollers in a headscarf and a cigarette in her mouth. Ken pulls up outside in his Rover.

Mom's crying and I'm crying and Marge takes one look at me and covers her mouth with her hand.

'Sweet bloody Jesus!'

'It's her tongue, Marge.'

Marge grabs Mom by the arm and shoves her towards the car.

'Don't wait for the ambulance, Sheila. Get in! Ken'll drive you. In! In! I'll stop with the kids.'

I sit on Mom's lap and Ken zooms away.

At the hospital I'm on a wheely bed and then, all of a sudden, I'm in a very white room under the brightest lights in the world and loads of nurses are holding my arms and legs and my head.

The thing that really makes me scream is the doctor trying to get his whole hand in my mouth. Someone is holding my chin and he keeps sticking something into my tongue and pulling it. My screams are coming from my belly and my nose because there's no room to let it out of my mouth. When he's finished, one of the nurses gives me a pink drink and tells me not to swallow but to spit it out, but I can't swallow anything because I'm crying so much.

They take me home after ages and ages and Mom sleeps with me all night in Dean's bed. She keeps stroking my hair and asking me if I'm all right and I just nod.

In the morning, Mom helps me come downstairs because my legs feel funny as well as my mouth. She sits me at the kitchen table and Dad shakes his head.

'What you was doing on the table, eh?'

'Don't make her talk, Arthur! Look at her mouth.' She pulls my chin and I have to open my big swollen lips and show him my tongue.

He winces and looks away.

'Six stitches, Arthur. They said she nearly bit it off altogether.'

She opens the fridge and takes out a block of ice cream in a blue-and-white-striped packet. She cuts a massive slice and puts it on a saucer in front of me with a teaspoon.

Tracey stands next to me and looks at my saucer. 'Can I have some?'

'No!' says Mom. 'Not unless you've bitten your tongue off as well. Have you? No? Didn't think so.'

Dad looks at Tracey. 'What you both was doing?'

'We were just playing, Dad, and then Mandy went on the table to sing "I can't get no satisfaction".'

Dad throws back his head and brays like a horse. He can hardly talk for laughing. 'You get some satisfaction now, ain't it, Mandy?'

One day, I'm in the garden playing with Karen in the pram.

'Give me a kith,' I say to her and when the

others hear they start to copy me, chasing me around the garden with a sing-song chant.

'Kit, kit, kit,' they say and add it to the list of my names: Skins, Patches, Minty, Kit.

7

It's Thursday night and we've been to the meeting. Conrad, a coloured boy who comes home with us from school for Mom to look after, came with us. Conrad is coming to our house more and more, and doing things like staying overnight. He's two years older than Kim and taller than everyone except Dad.

We pile into the kitchen, hungry after the long walk home from the bus stop. Kim says she'll make some porridge.

'Remember Black Nana's porridge?' I say. 'Remember the lumps?'

'Yeah, she used to make porridge for me as well when we lived in the West Indies,' says Conrad.

'Who did?' I ask.

'Nana. Chrissie.'

'You mean Black Nana?'

'Yeah.'

'How do you know Black Nana?' I ask.

He frowns and looks from one face to another. 'She's my granny as well.'

There's nothing for a while. Not a sound. Then the questions start, all of us piling in, crowding round him, and when he tells us that he's our brother, that he came to England from St Kitts when he was six, that his mom and my dad are his parents and that they had him in the West Indies before any of us were born, that he's as scared of Dad as we are, we all start laughing. It's one of the most exciting days of my life, of all of our lives. Of course he's my brother, I always knew, I never knew. He's part of me and I am part of him.

'Why didn't you tell us?' I ask.

'I thought you knew,' he says. And then he tells us about Black Nana, his nana.

'She loved me, spoiled me rotten. Me and my mother used to visit her and she'd cook great big dinners for us.'

I imagine Black Nana holding Conrad's hand maybe, smiling maybe, waving her son off to England and then waiting. All the time thinking, 'Any day now, Arthur will send for Conrad and send for his girlfriend, Catherine, and they can be a family again.'

But five years later when Dad sends home for someone to come to England, it's for her. And he's only asking because he wants her to come over and look after some white woman's half-black children, who don't want Black Nana around.

And I think of Conrad's mother, the quiet, pretty black woman who used to come and collect Conrad from our house. That woman is my dad's ex-girlfriend, the one he left behind with a one-year-old baby, who has to come calling round to our house and thank my mother for looking after her son while she goes to work.

Conrad comes and goes. He is part of us. He comes in without knocking. He gets older and more handsome. He gets tough and manly and as big as my dad. He visits with beautiful girls who hang on his every word. He talks about football with Dad and takes Dean to the Blues.

We watch *Carry On* films on a Saturday when Dad is out and laugh together.

He is always in our hearts.

8

'Fish and chips!' Mom bellows up the stairs. Excited voice. Without warning.

We hardly ever have fish and chips.

That Friday night after she bellows up the stairs, she goes to the fish-and-chip shop and comes back with Lorraine.

We are hungry and we are waiting.

'Where is she?' I ask no one, everyone.

Eventually, we give up. But then the front door opens and we tumble over one another to dash out to the hall. Mom is there in the porch and a girl is with her.

The girl is older than us, with long hair and freckles. She is crying and her two front teeth are crooked. The chips are nowhere to be seen.

'Go and watch the telly,' Mom hisses and shoos us away. She closes the door to the kitchen and that's that. Dad barely turns his head when we slink in, starving, and find somewhere to sit. I snuggle in between Kim and Tracey; their warmth will have to fill me up.

In the morning, she's still in our house, the girl with the crooked teeth. She's sitting in the kitchen with an empty plate in front of her so she's probably had toast, which probably means there's no bread left. I hurry to the packet and quickly spread margarine on the last two pieces, fold them in half and gobble them down.

'This. Is. Lorraine,' Mom says as I chew.

'Hello,' I say and smile with the bread stuck in the gap between my teeth.

'This is Mandy. Number two.'

Lorraine holds out her hand like I'm a grown-up.

'Don't stare,' says Mom. 'Tell the others to get up.'

When I go back to tell Tracey about the girl, I realize that Dean has been sleeping in our room on the floor.

'Mom said get up.' I throw the blankets off Dean. Kim is asleep and that's so normal I don't even try to rouse her. I sit on our bed and whisper to Tracey.

'That girl's downstairs.'

'From yesterday?'

'Lorraine, that's her name.'

Tracey is scratching her eczema. 'Why?' she says.

'I don't know. She's really pretty.'

'I know. I saw her.'

'She's eaten all the bread,' I lie. I can't be blamed.

Me and Tracey go downstairs to the kitchen to look at the girl.

Mom's found a new way of speaking for Lorraine.

'. . . yes, all five of them in nine years. I don't recommend it, Lorraine. I always wanted children, the more the better, but they're expensive. And Arthur wants to go home. Saves every penny. So we're a bit pinched here. But you're welcome, love. I know what it's like to be thrown out for love.' She sniffs as an invitation to Lorraine to ask her to continue.

But Lorraine is slow and Mom has to continue without the prompt.

'After we fell in love . . .'

Tracey side-eyes me.

'After we fell in love, me and Arthur, my mother threw me out. I'm Irish, you see. She didn't want a daughter who went with a black man. So I had to move in with Arthur. One room in a shared house. Kim was born there.'

She's off again, wafting in a pink haze down memory lane.

That summer Lorraine reads us stories at bedtime, and all the while her belly gets bigger and bigger.

She tucks me and Kim in one night and sees me looking at the massive bulge in front of her. I can't believe there is a curled-up baby in there.

'He'll be out soon. You can hold him if you like,' she says.

'I don't want to have babies,' I say. 'I don't want them to unravel me.'

'What?'

'I don't want them to undo the knot and unravel me.'

'Do you know how babies come out?' she says.

'Yes. Through your belly button. They undo the knot and unravel your skin, then tie it up again. I saw it on a programme.'

Lorraine is smiling when she pulls the blankets up around my neck.

'Babies come out between your legs,' she says.

She kisses my forehead and pats the blanket. 'Night night.'

When she's gone, I think about last year when my mom was pregnant with Karen.

The size of that baby was massive and it would be literally impossible for it to come out of the tiny hole where the wee comes out. I feel sorry for Lorraine. Someone should tell her the truth.

One day, when I'm coming up the road from school, I see Lorraine standing by the front door.

'Hello, love,' she says, but she looks straight past me, craning her neck up and down the street. I walk into the kitchen and Mom shakes her head.

'She'll make herself ill.'

Suddenly Lorraine hurries down the hallway, one hand on her belly. 'I can see him!' she cries.

I dash back to the front gate where she now stands smoothing her dress over her belly, her face fully alive. She's waving at a man in full sailor uniform, a navy hat on the back of his head. He's got a tight, rolling walk.

'Dougie!' she shouts and starts to wave. He waves back and nods as if to say, 'I see you!'

Then she's out of the gate and waddling down Springfield Road, and he's caught her round the shoulders and kissing her for all the neighbours to see. Mom is standing at the front door with a tea towel in her hand and tears in her eyes.

'Ah!' she says. 'Look at that.'

He shakes Mom's hand. 'Dougie,' he says.

Tracey and me nudge each other because we know this is a big moment in Lorraine's life.

'Come in, come in, come in,' Mom says.

They walk hand in hand, past me and Tracey at the gate, into the front room where nobody ever goes, and Mom shushes me into the kitchen, flapping the tea towel like I'm a fly at a picnic.

'Who is he?' I ask.

'He's the mistake she made, love. He's heartache.'

Dougie takes Lorraine away after she has their baby boy. He gets them a flat somewhere far away and I have to imagine what the baby will look like when he grows up, and if his teeth will fold over at the front like Lorraine's.

One day, much later, a letter comes and Mom reads it up by the front door.

'Oh, Lorraine,' she says and starts to cry. Dad asks her what's wrong, and she sniffs her way through the wedding and Lorraine making it up with her mother and the baby boy dressed as a page and Lorraine saying thank you for everything, and then she stops suddenly.

'I'm an idiot. She never even invited me.' She folds the letter up, puts it in the pocket of her apron and pushes past Dad on her way to hang out the washing.

He shakes his head and says the usual. 'You mother is a crazy woman.'

9

After Lorraine leaves, Mom gets a new job. She cleans the new mini-market on Stratford Road every afternoon after she collects Karen and Dean from school.

She comes home with dented tins and opened packets that she's got at a reduced rate.

Between five o'clock and six o'clock every night she's completely idle for one whole hour, which adds up to seven hours every week when she's not earning, and she tells us it's important she keeps bringing the money in. So she finds something to do with her leisure time, and that's cleaning the launderette. We never mind about going to the Laundrama to help Mom. The Laundrama smells of clean, of freshness, of order and properness.

We would never take our washing to the Laundrama. It costs too much money. We do our washing in the wash house at the back of our house between the kitchen and the garden.

When the washing is still damp, Mom always makes us carry it with us to the Laundrama in big carrier bags to be dried.

As soon as we walk in, one of us flips the sign from 'Open' to 'Closed' and the game starts, the hunt for lost coins. They are mostly under the dryers, a sixpence or thruppence that someone dropped or couldn't reach.

What we find, we keep. Dean always levers himself down behind the machines and the rollers because he's the size of a big pixie. That's where the most coins roll so he always ends up with the most money.

While she's cleaning and mopping, Mom pops our clothes in the warmest dryer and gets one of us to find her a lost coin to make it start.

Sometimes when we get there, other women are just finishing up and, because Mom knows everyone, she spends half her time saying hello and gossiping. There's a sort of party atmosphere, the folding and unfolding of arms, nudges, whispered things about men and hussies, who's been eating hot bread and is already showing.

'Give us a song, Dean, love,' says Hilda.

'Go on!' says Betty.

He clambers up on to the big dryers and stands there with his hands on his hips. His hair curls up at all angles, his arms are skinny, snappable. He's wearing red summer sandals that he's outgrown and Mom has done her usual trick of taking a Stanley knife to the front, cutting away an inch of leather so his toes can peek out. His smile is wide and confident.

'"It's Not Unusual"!' I shout and he nods like a Las Vegas crooner being handed the mic. He opens his arms wide and starts. He knows all the words, all the moves. The women are clapping and laughing and shaking their heads.

'Oooh, he's so good!'

'Little heartbreaker, he is.'

'You'll have to keep your eye on this one, Sheila.'

Even we, who have seen his routines dozens of times, have to stop and watch. He hops over the gaps between the machines, slipping on the metal. He struts to the end of the run and sashays back, working his way through the song, working his way through the women, right to the last note. But there's barely a beat before he segues seamlessly into Johnny Cash, Gene Pitney, Adam Faith.

Mom stops her jobs and we all gather round, looking up at the boy child as he prances and dances, word perfect, until, at the end of our concert, when the audience has gone home, he has sixpences and sweets and a bellyful of adoration.

10

We're waiting for Mom outside the Irish shop on Stratford Road. She's buying the things we will eat at Nan's, who can't be expected to put up with a whole tribe of us being hungry as well as poor as well as half black. So Mom always brings a shopping bag of stuff that she places on Nan's kitchen table.

Margaret Doyle, or Nan, is as neat as a pin, like the tall Edwardian house she shares with Grandad in the Irish part of town, the many rooms tidy and empty now her children are gone.

We know we are not in the same league as our white cousins, the children of Greta, of Michael, of Jimmy, Kevin or Mary, who have had the Catholic decency, at least, to marry of their own kind. We hardly see them. They must visit on other days when we're not expected, not wanted.

Nan always finds something for our brown fingers to do that's useful, endless and silent. Her favourite thing is the button box. She makes us sit on the floor and we have to tidy it, wind the threads neatly on themselves and put the needles on card in size order. And when we finish, we stack the buttons, big to small, into little piles that we call 'cakes', using a pearl or a black bead for the top.

As soon as the button box comes out, Grandad reaches for his accordion, puts the leather strap over his shoulder and rests the box on his knee like a baby.

'We'll have a song now,' he says.

He eases into something beautiful, 'The Wild Colonial Boy', 'The Patriot Game' or 'I'll Take You Home Again, Kathleen', songs we have heard from him all our lives.

In the summer, Nan shoos us into the garden so that she can take Mom inside for tea and gossip.

No matter how hard it is, Mom knows that she needs to tell her mother about the good news of the Kingdom and try to save her from Catholicism.

She starts at an oblique angle.

'Did you see there was an earthquake in India, Mom? It was on the news.'

'I did.'

'They're coming quicker now, aren't they? There's always some disaster somewhere in the world.'

'And there always was,' says Nan, because she knows every move on the chessboard.

'After Armageddon we won't have any more wars or conflict. And sickness as well. And old age. And there'll be lots of food for everyone. Don't you think that's lovely?' It comes out in a begging voice, a child who wants her mother's love.

'Armageddon now, is it?' says Nan.

'Yes, Jehovah's organization gives us warnings. It's all in *The Watchtower.*'

'Ah, Sheila,' says Nan, 'you shouldn't believe everything you read. Paper never refused ink.'

It's a push-me-pull-you of a dance, old as time, the child who was never the favourite, the mother who couldn't love enough. They lock in with clumsy footsteps, each one trying to lead, stepping on toes.

11

One Sunday, when I am eleven, we walk from the Kingdom Hall around the corner to Nan's house. Mom is bursting to tell her the news.

'Aidan's asked the girls to be bridesmaids,' she says.

Nan makes a pot of strong tea in the big brown pot and puts it on the table.

My mother takes her cup of tea and she's a different woman sipping it. Proud, she is. This will be a big affair: the last wedding of the Doyles, the youngest boy and my mother's favourite. She was fifteen when Aidan was born and she'd practically brought him up.

When she told Dad the day before, she picked her words carefully.

'They'll be bridesmaids, Arthur. It's lovely of him to ask the girls, isn't it?'

We already knew Dad's views on public occasions. His advice always centred on his one maxim: 'You better behave. You have the eyes of the white man on you.'

Nan is quick to pour cold water on my mother's joy.

'What about the dresses? They'll not be cheap,' she says with narrowing eyes.

'Aidan's paying for them. The girls have got to go to Northfield to get measured and there's a seamstress making them up.'

'I see,' Nan sniffs.

'And there's little pink muffs,' Mom continues undaunted.

'And shoes?' Nan is quick to pounce on my mother's pause. 'Shoes, Sheila,' she says, rapping the table. 'Have you told your husband they'll need shoes? White ones.'

Mom nods. 'I know.'

Nan lays a motherly hand on her daughter's arm.

'Leave it with me, Sheila.'

Mom's quiet on the way home, caught as she is between the meanness of her husband and the shame of having to take her mother's help. She often tells us the names her mother called her when she learned of her pregnancy with a black man. She counts off by unfolding her fingers one at a time. 'Whore. Dirty bitch. Disgrace. Prostitute. Jezebel. Tramp . . .'

Nan's rare visits to our house are on the strict understanding that my father will be at work, that she won't have to sit down with the beast and make conversation. Occasionally she gets it wrong and Dad comes home when she's still drinking tea in the kitchen, and when she hears him in the hall, she stands and buttons her coat.

'I have to be going now, Sheila. The bus.'

'Maggie,' my father says when he sees her. 'You keeping all right?'

'Oh yes,' she says, taking the long passage at a trot, barely breathing until she's safely out on Springfield Road waving goodbye.

Months go by. Our pink satin dresses hang upstairs under cellophane. Our little pink muffs dangle from silky pink cord. No shoes.

A few weeks before the wedding, Nan arrives, breathless, in the kitchen.

'Didn't I tell you I'd find something for the girls?'

Mom makes Nan a cup of tea in a proper cup.

'Thanks, Mom,' she says with her hand splayed over her heart.

We gather round as Nan opens her shopping bag. There are no shoeboxes, just plastic bags wrapped around something inside. She passes each bundle carefully to Mom.

'I went to the Rag Market,' Nan continues. 'If you can't find a bargain in that place, there's none to be had.'

Mom unwraps each package in turn and places the contents on the table in front of her. These are not shoes. These are gym shoes. They are second-hand. They are dirty and grey and scuffed and laceless and worn down at the back.

Nan looks from the shoes to Mom's face and back to the shoes.

'They'll do, they'll do. Sure, aren't the dresses long enough to cover them? Nobody will see them, Sheila. They're grand, aren't they?'

The next day, Mom shouts us all awake and tells us to get dressed. Excited voice, strong and certain.

'Hurry up! We're going into town. Shopping!'

We walk straight into Start-Rite.

'I want four pairs of white shoes,' she says confidently. 'It's for a wedding. They're going to be bridesmaids.'

My shoes are new, they are glittery and princess white with a pretty bow at the front. Tracey's are the same and because Kim is older, hers are a bit different, with a little heel. Karen's are pretty and dainty with glitter and a single pearl button. They cannot be passed from one girl to the next. They cannot be worn for school. We walk proudly out of the shoe shop, each of us swinging our own bag.

Only when we get home and Mom tells Dad how much it all cost do we realize the depth of the insult that Nan had dealt him.

'Good,' he says. 'Go tell Maggie the price.'

12

Everywhere else in the world it's Christmas. At 70 Springfield Road it's Wednesday 25th December. There are things we mustn't say, words that will earn us a slap or a lecture, a scripture or a look. The words are:

Christmas

Virgin Mary

Saviour

Mistletoe

Presents

Turkey

Wise Men

Donkey

Joseph

Manger

Fairy

Star

Bethlehem

Tree

Hallelujah

Hymn

Carols

Church

Mass

Hosanna

Tinsel

Excitement

The house is entirely and completely empty of decorations, tree, presents, smells of cinnamon and mulled wine, warmth, fun, extra food, games and relatives.

My father, who is not a Jehovah's Witness, makes enough Christmas cake to feed the whole of exiled St Kitts.

He loads the parcels of cake and us into the back of his car and skids us through the winter streets to drop them off one by one.

'Come in, come in! Yes, come!'

We stand politely while Dad talks to his friends from back home. Don't touch, don't speak, don't eat anything even if it's offered, don't interrupt.

We listen to the same repeated stories about back home, where the sun shone and you felt it in your bones.

'Bless you, Arthur,' an old woman says. 'You never forget us, Arthur. All year we look out for you.'

Every year, around New Year, Mom gets all dressed up to go to the Talk of the Town with her brothers and sisters. It's dancing and dinner and a band and a comedian and more dancing, Mom with her sister Teresa doing the jive because she can still move, you know.

Sometimes Mom's brothers will bring their wives, but Mom doesn't even bother to ask Dad any more. There would be no point.

Late afternoon, she sends me across the road to Marg.

'Mom said can she borrow some make-up. She's going to the Talk of the Town.'

Marg always has a cigarette in her mouth or between her fingers and has the make-up bag waiting by the front door.

'Crimson Dream, that lipstick is. Brand new. Tell her I've put the black pencil in instead of the brown because you need a bit of drama at night.'

Mom sits in the kitchen and assembles everything. I sit opposite to watch. She sits with a little mirror and takes her time with the eyeliner and lipstick.

Dad winks at us.

'You out to get yourself a fancy man, Sheila?'

'Might,' she says with a bitterness we've begun to expect. She's always tired these days and doesn't play along with Dad's jokes.

She shrugs on her coat, adds a little fur collar and snaps her handbag shut.

'I'll get a taxi back,' she says boldly, willing him to object. He says nothing, avoiding the inevitable row.

'Bye, then!' she calls from the front door and we watch her sashay down Springfield Road, off to the bright lights of Five Ways.

We're all still up when she comes home, tipsy.

'Got a proper black cab,' she says and winks in our direction, because she knows Dad will hate it. He barely turns his head, but we watch her – slightly giddy, lighter somehow, all her edges blurred by Baileys Irish Cream.

She staggers out of the room and up to bed, singing, 'Please release me, let me go.'

In the morning, she'll take two Panadol.

13

No school for the summer holiday.

Mom's become a childminder. The doorbell starts ringing at seven in the morning with people dropping their children off. Mom peels swaddled babies out of their mothers' arms with a practised twist.

Me, Kim and Tracey have to feed and wash the babies, bring the wind up, stop them crying, jiggle them on our hips.

But on Saturdays and Sundays, when all the kids have gone, we get our house back and Mom orders us outside: anywhere will do – the garden, someone else's garden – just don't be inside under her feet.

I tiptoe to the front garden to sit on the wall.

I sit on the front-garden wall for hours.

Here comes Maggie May, the oldest woman in the world, striding down the road with a feather in her magnificent hat. When she passes, she tosses her long grey curls.

'I am to the shops the day,' she says, not exactly to me but there isn't anyone else.

Then just at the curve of the road, there's a new person I've never seen before, a tramp. He is bent over, grasping a short wooden walking stick. He's in dark-brown rags, wearing massive shoes like Charlie Chaplin, and he has coats on top of coats and a scarf that is mostly tears and holes.

He's so bent I can't see his face, but he's coming close. I retreat into the front garden to let him go past, but he doesn't pass. He stands at the gate and comes towards me.

I back off into the house.

'Mom! Mom!'

She comes from the kitchen with a tea towel in her hand.

'Hello,' she says and has the read of him immediately.

'Missus,' he replies, 'would you have a drink of water?'

'Come in. Sit down.'

I look at her. She's just mopped the hall and kitchen and this man smells like a bin. We don't know him. Why does she do this? She's always talking to people who don't need talking to, strange people or mad people who everyone else avoids.

He shuffles through and I follow in his wake. The stench is unholy. He sits just inside the kitchen door with his legs spread, both hands on his stick. His face is filthy.

'Or a cup of tea,' he says.

My mother whistles and hums and I dash past the old man and into the garden.

'There's a tramp in the kitchen!'

We crowd around the back door. Even from here we can smell him. We watch Mom give him a cup of tea. She makes him a sandwich with food she has bought for us. She cuts it in half and hands it to him on a plate, but he whips it off and stuffs the whole thing in his mouth and starts muttering.

'Have you come a long way?' she asks, folding her arms.

We catch the odd word. They are all 'fuck'.

As he drinks his tea, he eyes her through the filthy slits above his nose. 'Have you got a shilling, missus?'

She takes her purse out and hands him a coin. 'What's your name?'

'Morgan,' he says. 'I sleep where I sit.'

We take a collective gasp. Could she go so far as to let him sleep, to let him stay like the children who she looks after? Could she let him stink out the entire house and eat all our food?

'Well,' she says. 'I've got my jobs to do today, Mr Morgan. I'll help you up.'

He takes ages to stand, huffing, puffing and swearing. He hands her the mug and shuffles off down the hallway.

'He stinks, Mom,' I say.

'Not everyone can have a bath whenever they want. One day you can have everything and the next day, bad luck strikes.'

She opens all the windows and wafts a tea towel around the kitchen.

'Out! Out!' she says. 'Go and play.'

He comes back, Mr Morgan, every couple of months. Mom gives him tea in a cup that none of us will ever touch again and a sandwich on a plate that is dead to us.

The end comes when me and Dean are in the kitchen and Mom is tidying up. Mr Morgan is on the chair by the door. He looks at us for a long time as he chomps through his food.

'Whose are the niggers?' he asks.

'What did you say?' says Mom.

'The little niggers. Who do they belong to?'

My mother walks over to him and brings him to his feet.

'Up you get,' she says. She walks him to the front door and slams it behind him.

She takes his mug and plate into the garden and smashes them against the brick wall.

'Cheeky sod,' she says.

14

The only reason we go to Waverley Grammar School is because Dad wouldn't let Kim go to Dame Elizabeth Cadbury, the art school that offered her a scholarship.

'Art? You can't do nothing with drawing,' he says when the letter arrives.

The only grammar school with a space for Kim is Waverley Grammar School on the other side of the city, two long bus journeys away. And where Kim goes, I must follow. But this morning, I have to make my way by myself.

I walk to the bus stop at the bottom of the road with my satchel and PE bag. It's raining this morning.

The bus comes sizzling along the wet road and I hop on.

Mom tells us all about how she used to let her friends off with their fares when she was a conductress. She used to work at the same depot as my dad.

'He was just like a film star,' she says. 'The best-looking man I'd ever seen.' She made sure she worked the same shifts as he did, then sat with him in the canteen and then became his friend. She must have worn him down.

I get off at Camp Hill and have to cross the busy dual carriageway to catch the next bus that takes me to Small Heath. Dad told me to always walk to the crossing, but it's a hundred yards away and I'm so tired.

I wait at the edge of the pavement. Cars rush past, lorries thunder by and I stand back so I don't get splashed, watching the lights change from green to amber, then red. But there's hardly a gap before the next load of cars come and I have to run really quickly.

I am a foot from safety when the pale-green Ford Anglia hits me. Out of the corner of my eye, with a somersault heart, I see it following the curve of the road. I pull my satchel to my chest like it might save me. I watch my PE bag drop under the wheel and then I'm light as a feather, spinning up and losing everything and worrying in that airborne instant, will I be late, will my pumps get run over?

I come down on my right side, hard, and scuff my forehead on the dirty concrete. I hear the van brake and car doors slam.

'Don't move her!' a man shouts.

I close my eyes and try to turn my head but I can't. I am crying and a woman says, 'Shhhh. The ambulance is coming.'

'I didn't see her. I didn't see her. I didn't see her.'

He sounds so young. There are other men telling him it's not his fault and I want to nod and agree, but my neck hurts and one of my legs feels like it's not there. Over all of it, my hip is thudding and I want to turn my body over and get my weight off it.

'Don't move,' says the woman.

'The crossing's right there,' says someone else. 'I didn't see her,' he says again.

I'm sitting up in bed on the children's ward when Mom comes. I can see she's been crying.

I'm so glad to see Mom that I try to smile but it comes out wrong and I'm crying again. I've got a plaster on my forehead and a bandage on my arm.

'We don't think she needs an X-ray,' says the nurse, patting Mom and not me. 'She only got clipped by the car, luckily. We'll keep her in – bang on the head, can't be too careful.'

All Mom can do is swallow and blink and hold my hand while the nurse talks to her.

The nurse moves close in to Mom and drops

her voice. 'He's outside,' she says, 'the young man who hit her. We had to give him something for the shock. Pale as death, he was. Poor thing. He said he wouldn't leave until he'd spoken to you.'

I start crying harder now, because I know what Mom's like when someone does something to one of us.

I keep pulling her hand until she looks away from the nurse. 'It was my fault, Mom. Don't tell him off.'

But the nurse takes Mom away and I have to wait ages until she comes back.

'What a lovely boy,' she says. 'He's had such a shock. He looks terrible.'

Eventually, she gives me a kiss and goes home.

The next morning, Mom helps me hobble outside. And there, waiting for us, is Dad in the car. He leans behind him and opens the door so I can get in.

'What I tell you?' he says.

'I didn't see the car,' I answer.

'It see you, though, ain't it?'

I cry quietly in case I make him angry.

'We've got to keep an eye on her, Arthur, and if anything changes we have to bring her back in.'

'I tired. Tell these children,' he says as he drives away. 'Tired.'

In a few days I'm well enough to go back to school. I don't have to do PE for weeks.

There are six black children in the whole school. Me and Kim are two of them. I'm nearly two years younger, and yet I follow her only a year behind.

I'm clever and near the top in nearly every lesson, but I don't do more than the minimum, even in English.

Mom always goes to Parents' Evening alone. Dad says he's working. She puts on her best coat. We have to wait at home.

When she comes back, she has my report and stands in the door of the telly room to tell Dad what the teachers said.

'You wouldn't think it was Mandy's Parents' Evening, Arthur. It was Kim this and Kim that. They hardly talked about Mandy. She's top in everything.'

'Who?' says Dad.

'Kim.'

'What them say?'

'The English teacher said she writes lovely poems and she's brilliant at Biology. But Art is her best subject.'

'Mandy?'

'No, Arthur. Kim.'

I drift upstairs and leave Mom talking to the side of my dad's face while he watches *News at Ten*.

15

The house smells of Bay Rum.

The men are coming.

I pour KP Nuts into never-used glass bowls and place them on the glass coffee table in the middle of the front room. The men are coming.

Mom wears a yellow dress with big green roses on the skirt. She knows these men from her first days with Dad. The men who didn't go with white women, who married the women they brought over, the glossy black women with proper hairdos and cookery skills.

She tells us stories about the men when Dad is out.

'Judas didn't get a name like that for nothing. And Stump? All smiles now but not when I knew him.'

'Stump!'

'Judas!'

'Sugar!'

'Harry!'

'Grumble!'

'George!'

Dad slouches downstairs with his easy walk

and immaculate self. He looks in the hallway mirror. He licks a finger and smooths it over his eyebrows. His swagger is a front. We know without being told that he's nervous. These are the men from home, from the boat and his first days in England. Made-good men.

We clutter the narrow hallway as they come, shaking hands and easing past one another into the best room. The noise thrills, the accents, knowing that for a moment we are like everyone else, like people who have visitors and nuts in bowls.

'Lord! Look Tracey! She big, eh? How big you is, Tracey?'

'No, no, Sugar! You mad? This is Kim, isn't it? Kim?'

I'm examined for my skinniness and my Indian looks.

'And this is Mandy! She meagre, eh? She look like a cha-cha man child, don't it?'

My mother hates this. Tries her best to smile at the long-running joke.

'You sure this one is yours, Lofty?' says Sugar, cuffing me under the chin.

My father laughs as I try to stand behind him. 'You don't see the gap in her teeth, Sugar? Me no worry.'

It's Stump I like best. He has a wide smile and

a goatee beard that bobs up and down when he laughs, and he's always laughing. He's the one who always notices my mother when the others don't.

'Sheila,' he says, 'you good?' He claps his hands.

When the door closes, we wait outside in the fragrant space they've left behind. It's all muffled in the front room. There are long sentences in Kittian patois – St Kitts slang. There are long run-ups to the jokes. There are yells and the rumble of Stump's deep voice and then BOOM! The laughter of a hundred voices.

So goes the afternoon and into the evening, but they never stay late. These men were really going somewhere else, but they have stopped off to see their friend, the one who never goes out, the one who keeps himself apart, not a drinker, hardly a gambler, not a womanizer or a dancer.

If they want to see Lofty, they have to come to him, so they do, for old times' sake. Now, the goodbyes are long in the making, a huddle up by the front door and a last joke, and waving and waving until the cars pull away and the house is dead again.

Dad never leaves with them but that evening – perhaps because he's had a tot of rum and because maybe there's a little bit of regret that he said no, again, and because some days he wishes he was one of the boys, and because sometimes the sunless country and the relentless white man get him down – he goes down to the bus depot for a game of cards.

He pulls on his overcoat.

'Sheilo?' he calls but doesn't wait for an answer. 'I going out to come back.'

He never takes her with him. Never sticks his elbow out for her, never holds her coat. In all my life, they never leave the house together and stroll down Springfield Road arm in arm. They leave at separate times, for separate things, to separate places.

16

It is my birthday. I am fourteen. I wake up and tell Tracey.

'Happy birthday,' she whispers.

The closest I can come to imagining birthday presents is by getting out the Littlewoods catalogue. We linger on each page and imagine what it would be like to have an Etch A Sketch or KerPlunk.

Dad comes in with a surprised look on his face, a happy look, proud and excited at the same time.

'Come look,' he says.

We follow him out to the front of the house. He's standing by a massive car in silver and navy blue, the best car I have ever seen.

'Princess 3 litre, Vanden Plas. Look inside. Get in.'

We slide into the back seat and he points it all out to us: the little walnut tables that fold out of the leather like magic; the chrome ashtray with a special button that makes the ash vanish; armrests that disappear back from whence they came.

Mom stands on the front step.

'You bought a new car, Arthur?' she says.

'Look good, don't it?' he answers. 'Come, we go for a spin.'

She looks at him in his good suit and his good shoes, proud and excited and asking her for once in her life to go out with him for a little drive, and she turns and goes inside. She sits at the kitchen table and starts adding up the catalogue money she's been collecting for weeks.

Eventually, she folds the notes and puts the coins in an envelope. She sighs loud and long.

'A new car. There's me working all hours God sends and handing my money over so he can buy a new car. You're a bloody idiot, Sheila.'

The next week, Mom buys herself a harmonica. She buys herself a Davy Crockett-style fur hat. Every day, she sits on the back step wearing her hat in the shade and learning the harmonica with her eyes closed.

Over and over she goes, breathing in and out so there are no gaps in the tune, and every so often, she drops it away from her mouth and hums or sings under her breath to remind herself of the notes. 'Beautiful dreamer, wake unto me . . .'

*

The next day, they're arguing. Dad's diabetes is out of control. It took months for them to diagnose his losing weight, his tiredness, but no one is surprised it's diabetes, the thing that killed Black Nana when she went home.

'I keep telling you, Arthur. You can't have Hermesetas in custard with a sponge pudding. You'll kill yourself the way you're going.'

'Then you all can bring me back, ain't it? The resurrection or whatever you call it.' He winks at me. 'I rise from the dead straight into paradise, isn't it, Sheilo? Diabetes done.'

'Don't make fun of it, Arthur. It's going to happen. It's in the Bible.'

'Oh, oh! In the Bible.'

She stops washing up and faces him. 'What about your paradise? You saving up every penny you earn and building that bloody house in St Kitts while this one falls down around our ears? I suppose that's all right, is it? Your kids in jumble-sale clothes while you stock up on suit lengths so you can strut around the West Indies.'

His face wears a terrible look. The house in St Kitts is his dream, his reason for being, his reason to work, his reason for coming here in the first place. And the reason he doesn't feed us and dress us, the reason he has to look good and be different and not go out and waste money on drink. The reason he breathes.

'I'm working my fingers to the bone and doing everything with my money while you're keeping yours to yourself,' she says.

Dad speaks quietly. 'When I come here, it was only to go back. I tell you that long time.'

'You've had kids since then, Arthur.'

'They can come.'

'And what about me? I suppose I'm not invited?'

'You can come if you want. I'm going home, Sheila. I tired tell you. I'm going home.'

'You make me sick,' she says under her breath, but we all hear.

Dad stands up. He towers over her, six foot six versus five foot two. 'My paradise will come before yours, Sheila.'

She starts to cry.

'If only I had a one-bedroomed flat,' she sniffs. 'I just want to live on my own. I've had enough.'

17

Now, there are days on end when Mom's in a bad mood. She goes to work as an auxiliary nurse at Dudley Road Hospital. She volunteers for every unpopular shift, every weekend night shift, Friday, Saturday, Sunday, eight at night until eight in the morning.

Her disappearing becomes more regular. She starts brushing her hair and finding excuses to go to the shop. She starts dropping a name into conversation, Ned, a neighbour down Passey Road, a nice man with a lovely front garden, a black man. It takes ages for us to understand.

One day, she sends me and Karen to the shop for some bread.

On our way down Passey Road, I see him, this tall man with a trilby, with a trowel and a white shirt open at the collar. He says hello when we pass and seems to recognize Karen. She waves at him.

On our way home, we pass him again. He's leaning on the gate this time.

'Sweet?' he says, rattling a paper bag.

We take one each and, as we stand there, he

tells us what he's planting: flowers for shade, flowers for colour, red and orange to remind him of home.

'Guyana,' he says. 'Beautiful country. How is your mother?'

I see my father in him, the yearning for home and the slow working of the jaw, but he's softer and rounder, scruffier as well. He's nice and seems really interested in us.

'She's fine, thank you.'

He goes as if to speak, to say something, but changes his mind.

'Say hello from me,' he says.

There's a sort of question in my mind about him but I can't reach it. Karen rushes home and tells Mom she saw Uncle Ned. Mom flushes red and looks at me with frightened eyes.

'It's OK,' I say, 'we only took one sweet each.' I think she's worried that we've disgraced her with our greed or bad manners, but she grabs her purse and is out of the door in a flash.

'I forgot to tell you to get some sugar.'

She's gone for ages and when she comes home she slumps into a kitchen chair and throws her purse on the table.

'What is it he says?' she asks me.

'Who?'

'Your father.'

'I don't know.'

'Yes, you do. "Your mother is a crazy woman." That's what he thinks of me, and he's right. What did I expect? All men are the same, aren't they? They're all promises and sunshine, but you still get wet, don't you? It's all bloody drizzle at the end of the day. I'm stupid, that's what I am.'

She makes a cup of coffee and sits staring out of the window, tears in her eyes.

Every so often, Mom will collect milk bottles. Three pints get delivered every day. She washes two bottles and puts them out the front for the milkman. The last one is placed outside the back door in a neat and tidy row. It goes on for weeks. Eventually she starts stacking them in an old plastic laundry basket. We watch it fill up with the empties. It's only a matter of time.

She waits until Dad's gone to work, then opens the back door and hauls the clanking laundry basket outside into the concrete yard.

She looks calm. She selects a milk bottle from the pile, picks it up and throws it with all her might against the wall of the outhouse and watches it smash into tiny pieces. She bites her tongue between her teeth and picks up another one and throws it again. We stare out of the upstairs window. You can smell the fight, hear her grunt and grunt and exhale as she works her way through the bottles, one after another, sweating, staring, single-minded. It makes a kind of music, the bottles and the sound of her fury. When the basket is empty, she goes inside and fetches the broom. She's fine then for a few days.

18

School ends. I'm overjoyed to be on the bus to Garretts Green Technical College. It's about as far away from home as possible without actually ending up in Coventry. Kate said she was going to do secretarial studies, so I signed up with her. Two weeks before the start of the course, she told me she wouldn't be going because she'd got taken on as a trainee with the National Westminster Bank.

I'm pleased for her. I'm disappointed. I'm angry. Kate, behind me in every single subject at school, ninth or tenth when I was first or second. But I can't get a job. Everything I apply for, from basic clerical to shop work in town, is a yes, yes, yes, come for an interview.

So I skip along to the office, clutching my exam certificates, with my best smile, but as soon as they see me it's the same thing.

'Mandy O'Loughlin?'

'Yes.'

'O'Loughlin?'

'Yes.'

'Isn't that Irish?'

'Yes, my mom's Irish but it's my dad's name.'

'Your dad?'

'Yes.'

'He's . . .'

'West Indian.'

'Right, right. Yes, well . . .'

Every time I slink back home, Dad talks to the black half of me who doesn't get the job: 'You can't trust the white man.'

And I have to sit silent, listening to the same speech that ends up the same way.

'You walk with an umbrella?'

'Yes, Dad.'

'You polish you shoe?'

'Yes, Dad.'

He kisses his teeth. 'They give the job to the white girl that come in after you.'

Room 2H is set up with desks in rows, every one dominated by a manual typewriter. Right by the door, near the plug socket, there is a single, ultra-modern electric IBM Font Ball typewriter, and a tall girl grabs it.

We are in ADVANCED secretarial studies.

The tall girl with the electric typewriter is Faye Mortimer. She's older than us, nineteen, with a tumble of creamy hair. She makes it plain at break time that she lived a life before she came back to college. She waitressed her way around

California and surfed the golden sands of Santa Cruz before she ran out of money.

Three of us are sitting around the impossibly glamorous older woman. She offers round her cigarettes and we all take one.

'I'm here for the fucking certificates,' she says, 'not to learn how to give head.'

I say nothing because I have no idea what the last part of the sentence means. But I too am here for the certificates, so I nod and cough on the strongest cigarette I have ever tasted.

I determine to part my hair down the middle and lose half a stone by next week.

*

Faye and I sit upstairs on the bus and have two fags each. Faye talks about guys, not boys, about scenes, not clubs or pubs.

We get off the bus and head up New Street towards the Town Hall. There's a narrow little alley between a boarded-up shop and a second-hand jeweller's, and she nips down there. I follow. In she goes through a green door with peeling paint and up some concrete stairs.

As she walks, she shouts, 'Hey, hey!' She pushes through some wired glass doors and along a corridor.

'Hey, hey!'

It's freezing and musty but at the end of the long walk there's an open door and music playing. We walk towards it and into a big room with metal shelves everywhere, like it was once an office.

The sun shines through dusty windows and on to a tall, white man, so thin his stomach is concave. He has the strangest hairstyle I have ever seen, shaved everywhere except the top, where bleached blond locks are piled up high. He's ironing a red silk shirt and singing along about a revolution that will not be televised.

Except he's not really singing, he's reciting the song like a poem.

I drop my bag and sit down on huge floor cushions covered with old carpet. Faye kisses the man and sits next to me. She puts a tin in my lap.

'Go on,' she says.

I open the tin. There's a khaki sort of loose tobacco inside and some cigarette papers. I look back at her.

'Give it here,' she says, smiling, and she splits open a cigarette, empties the tobacco on to a paper and sprinkles in some of the khaki stuff.

Faye passes me her new cigarette and pats her chest.

'Keep it down,' she says. 'The smoke, keep it down.'

It tastes half bitter, half sweet, and I close my eyes and concentrate on holding the warmth in my chest for as long as possible. When I breathe out, there's practically nothing there.

'Pass it to Max,' she says.

I pass it on and Max goes to the record player in the corner of the room and starts the same record all over again. He dances around with the sweet cigarette and every time the song says, 'The revolution will not be televised,' we all say it together and we pass the sweetness and we sing and we hold the sweetness inside and we sing until we are all shouting together, 'The revolution will not be televised!' and I start to laugh.

Faye is watching me with half-open eyes. And Max is putting on another record and beckoning me on to my feet. He pulls me up and starts doing a floaty dance.

'Golden Years, gold, whop, whop, whop . . .'

And the next sweet cigarette has come round to me and I'm dancing with David Bowie and Max on a Tuesday night and the sun shines on the dusty windows and the world is a very, very nice place.

When it's really black outside, Faye walks me to the bus stop.

'You're OK,' she says. It's not a question and I suck it down where I kept the sweet, sweet smoke.

The 91 takes me right to the end of the street and when I get off I stay at the bus stop for a few minutes, checking myself over.

I've got my bag. Yeah. I've got my shoes on. Yeah. And my coat. Yeah. Coat. Yeah. And my hair. Stop laughing, because nothing is funny. Ha ha ha ha. I'm OK. Act natural. All right, I'm home. I'm going to go inside and go upstairs. Straight upstairs. You can do it.

The house is quiet. I remember it's Tuesday. Everyone has gone to the meeting. Dad is watching the telly.

'You late!' he shouts without moving his head.

19

The best afro in college is owned by Mikey. He sits with the Engineering apprentices and wears a red check shirt and very well-pressed jeans. He notices me. I notice him. This has been going on for months. He's tall and skinny with a high bum and languid walk. He's not handsome. All his features are too big – but he has beautiful hands. He talks with his friends and glances over at me. He never smiles. Just glances over and sometimes nods.

Faye says she's had enough. 'He's one of them guys. All notes and no music.'

She hooks her fingers in her mouth and whistles. The whole canteen goes quiet. Everyone looks.

She gestures at me and points at him. 'Well? You gonna just sit there?' she shouts.

'Don't!' I hiss.

'What? He fancies you and you fancy him. What?'

He does nothing, doesn't even look embarrassed, but just as we're all going back to our classes, he sidles up to me.

'You're Mandy,' he says. 'I'm Mikey.'

'I know.'

He raises his eyebrows. 'That's the small talk done, then.'

Faye and the others hang back but I can hear them tittering.

'Your friend says you'd like to go out with me,' he says.

'She also said you're all notes and no music,' I reply, already at the limit of my banter.

'I'll meet you outside after,' he says. 'See if I can play you some tunes.'

'OK.'

Faye tells me to play it cool and he's lucky to get within half a mile of someone as good-looking as I am.

'I mean,' she says, 'he's punching well above his weight. He's pretty ugly.' No one disagrees.

He's waiting for me outside the main gate and we get the bus together, sitting on top with our cigarettes.

Mikey says he's asked people about me and knows I've got three sisters and a brother and an Irish mother. Says he's been watching me and likes what he sees. Likes my clothes and my hair and my wedge shoes. Likes the colour of my skin and the gap in my teeth. Likes the way I carry myself.

'You don't go on with slackness,' he says, and all this while he's looking straight ahead and not at me. He says everything like we're discussing a third person, like I might have an opinion on his research and say 'Well done' when he's finished.

We get off and walk the streets of the city centre, talking and looking in shop windows. We pass a girl laying into a cream cake, half of it in a paper bag, the other half in her mouth, and Mikey shakes his head.

'Don't walk and eat, man.'

Mikey tells me more about his rules for optimum behaviour and his plans for the future. He works in the office of a foundry in Smethwick; he designs parts for machines that make other machines. He's the apprentice and gets the shit jobs.

'Fuckers always taking the piss,' he says as we lean against the wall outside Virgin Records. 'But that job can't hold me. Mikey Douglas is better than that.'

'What are you going to do?' I ask.

'Get my own business. Get a Triumph Spitfire. Get a house in a good area. Get my own business. People can't hold Mikey.'

I notice now the perfection of him, the half-moon cuticles of his fingernails, the shine on his shoes, the smooth shine of his shave, the unbroken circumference of his afro.

We walk around for ages until we end up near my bus stop.

When the bus comes, he touches me for the first time. A little shove on my shoulder. He tells me we're going to the pictures on Saturday night. Says he'll meet me outside at half seven, The Gaumont. I don't say no.

It's the last day of term. I'm waiting at the bus stop with Faye; we're going to see Max to say goodbye. Faye's going to London to wait for her exam results. Then Heathrow.

'Then it's ciao to the land of grey,' she says.

Max's red silk shirt hangs by a nail, limp and threadbare.

'I know you won't fucking write, Faye,' he says, passing her the spliff, 'so don't even say you will.'

'Yeah? You should try having the energy to do anything after eighteen hours on your feet, bar to diner, bar to diner, bar to diner.'

It's the first time her adventures have taken on the pale colours of real life.

'And it's so expensive in San Francisco. I didn't eat some days. And Debbie turned out to be a bitch.'

'Could have told you that,' he says.

'Yeah, well. She took my bloke.' Faye forgets to pass the spliff on to me. 'And if I go back, I'm not even going to California. I've decided. New Mexico is where it's at.'

The 'if' sounds like thunder. She looks up suddenly. The cat is creeping out of the bag. Is this a glimpse of the truth? She snaps the bag shut.

'I mean, it was great and everything. I'm still going. Definitely. Yeah. But just to New Mexico, that's all.' She finally hands me the spliff and puts on a record. She starts swaying and singing. We smoke some more, play another few records, and I leave early. I kiss Faye goodbye.

'You're all right,' she says and holds me for a long time. 'I'll write.'

'Yeah, and I'll write back,' I say.

She tucks her weed tin in my hand. 'Look after yourself.'

I smoke the last two inches of my last spliff as I walk the long way to the bus stop. I'm eking out the spliff, letting it go out and lighting it again. The trees are an impossible green and the sun paints everything gold and bright.

Mikey didn't last long. The rules were too many and I couldn't keep up. I was always going to be less than his vision of me. But there's a pretty-looking mixed-race waiter in one of the hotels in town who always gives me the eye when I walk past.

I feel the whole world expand before me like a golden road that leads ever onward.

20

Kim is first to leave home. She's been listening carefully at the Kingdom Hall and when Brother Stannard said that the need was great in the north-east, she takes it to heart, packs her bags and says goodbye. She's doing God's work in Durham, and our mother can hold her head up at the meetings.

Me and Tracey have more or less stopped going to the meetings, finding excuse after excuse. Mom stands over us in our beds and cries about it.

'Why can't you be more like Kim? What's going to become of you when Armageddon comes?' I keep my eyes closed.

'Oh, Jehovah!' she says, raising her eyes to the ceiling. 'Help them understand!'

No lightning bolt breaks through the roof. The end of days, 1975, was two years ago. Jehovah's Witnesses got their sums wrong and we know it.

Mom is saving up in earnest to go to America, to get away from us, to get away from Dad.

She books herself a Miami flight to leave just before Christmas.

'I need some sun,' she says with a sniff, making sure Dad can hear.

'Bye, Mom!' we shout from the front door. Tracey and I look at one another, her departure fitting perfectly into our plans. She's gone for three months and, by the time she comes back, we are living in Handsworth in a rented house with two mattresses on the floorboards upstairs.

I stop temping in the banks and offices of the city centre and sign on the dole.

We lose weight. We gain friends. We reason into the early hours of the morning, learning about Haile Selassie and Marcus Garvey's fleet of Black Star liners. We spend our nights in blues and bars and shebeens, our days asleep. I become a master spliff builder, finding a simple, engrossing beauty in their construction, the perfect tip, the flat end with the tiny little twist of Rizla. There is not a day when I am not completely and magnificently stoned.

One day, there is a knock on the door. It's Kim. We hug and she steps inside and tells us about her ministry and the loneliness of Durham, how one day she woke up and knew she had to come home. She has left the Witnesses for good. She has lost the same thing we all have.

21

Madame Symanski rents out every spare room in her enormous Victorian villa in Moseley Village. I have a bedsit at the front of the house.

Upstairs, above me, lives Christian. He's an ex-student who never made it back home after his anthropology degree at Birmingham University. He wears a huge black trench coat with dull brass buttons and Dr Martens. Everything is too big for him – his clothes, his ideas, the world in general.

He walks his room all night, talking to himself, singing to himself, and Madame Symanski has to bang on his door and tell him to go to bed. Sometimes, he makes strange vegetarian balls of sticky brown rice that he places in some kind of mysterious pattern on a golden tray. He knocks on everyone's door and makes us take a particular one.

'That one is yours because I put essence of Boswellia in it for posture. You're bending wrong.'

'Yeah, thanks, Christian,' I say, careful to close

the door before he can come inside. Once, he didn't leave for two days and talked non-stop.

He always, always, always asks how you are and waits for an answer. And he is completely mad.

Every so often he goes home to his parents somewhere in Staffordshire and returns laden with food and money and gifts and clothes. He owns all this for exactly five minutes before his new friends, the thieving chancers of Moseley Village, come round and clean him out.

One day I hear the front door open. I'm freezing. I'm boiling. I'm getting some kind of fever. I've just had a bath across the corridor from my room.

I hear footsteps in the hallway and a cough. I pull the towel tight and peek round the corner. But I'm not peeky enough and there he is, smiling like a Mormon. Christian.

'Yeah, yeah, I had a bath this morning but the water started running cold,' he says, taking two giant steps towards me. He always starts midway through a conversation we haven't been having. I half trot to my room.

'Yeah, yeah, and then, yeah, went into the village . . .' Christian pushes open the door to my room and I scamper in. He leans on the door jamb, 'There you go, yeah.'

He's almost in the room now, carrying on without a pause. 'Saw Hughie just now, yeah, yeah. He's lost all his fucking gear, man. Robbed when he was sort of . . . you know Hughie. Anyway, Church Road or somewhere, yeah, I couldn't see him like that. Sort of pained me here.' He taps his chest where his big heart lives. 'Gave him my coat and keffiyeh and I had that scarf since I was in Palestine. I mean, yeah. But you know, I sort of had to.'

'Hughie? Fucking hell, you're an idiot, Christian,' I say, trying to close the door.

'Ah, yeah, I mean, yeah,' he says with his angelic face and watery eyes, 'it's my destiny. So, yeah, you know, me and you have talked about this before, yeah. If you—'

'Yeah, destiny, destiny. I remember. OK. Doesn't mean you've got to let people shit on you, Christian. You can still say no. And can you just . . .' I ease the door towards him. He smiles and shakes his head.

'She was always angry,' he whispers and backs away slowly. 'Turmoil.' In two strides he is halfway up the stairs. I watch him go, his jeans hanging off his backside, his jumper, mostly holes, covering the sharp bones of his back.

'What?'

90

He jumps over the banister and is in my room before I can move.

'Jezebel,' he says, folding his legs under him like a praying mantis as he concertinas down on to my floor cushions.

'Fucking hell, Christian.' I close the door and pull the blanket off my bed, hunching under it to get dressed.

'Yeah, yeah, she was in turmoil, that's what people didn't realize. Turmoil, yeah? People don't realize that her . . . her . . . ways, yeah, the way she behaved, was because she was angry and lost. She was you, yeah, yeah. You and her,' he says, knitting his hands together and showing me the evidence.

'Oh, I'm Jezebel?'

'Was, was.'

I stand over him, dripping hair, hands on still-damp hips. 'Don't tell me, Christian, reincarnation?'

He nods with his eyes closed. 'Yeah, yeah, she has passed to you.'

'And you've met her, like, when you were back there in biblical times?'

'Throughout, yeah.'

'Oh, right. Who were you then? John the Baptist?'

'Joseph of Arimathea,' he says, like he's giving his name to the dole office. 'Yeah, yeah. Had to step in and help with the burial of Christ. It was a day like today, actually. Chilly.'

I've been here before with Christian. I'm too ill to pretend I'm swallowing any of it.

'That's the thing about reincarnation, isn't it, Christian? Everybody is somebody.'

'Yeah, yeah, that's right,' he says, smiling, happy to have finally converted me. 'Everyone becomes somebody.'

'No, what I mean is, everyone is a queen, a courtier, Michelangelo's chisel maker, Da Vinci's sister. Can't remember the last time I heard one of you lot say, "I was a village idiot with no teeth." No. You're all a big someone or did the big something.'

I can't help but go on, the fever eating away at my patience and good manners.

'It's just another way of being special, Christian. You're no different from the Jehovah's Witnesses. "Oh, God only loves us. Just us. We're the chosen ones. We will be in paradise, you won't."'

I feel the rage of my childhood breaking through the water like a killer whale.

'And it would have been fucking grim to be

alive in those days, Christian, and you'd be dead at thirty.'

He slowly levers himself up.

'Sorry,' he says, but like it's me he's sorry for, not himself. He puts his hand on my shoulder and closes the door quietly afterwards.

I collapse on to the cushions, cocoon myself in the blanket and fall asleep.

*

I wake again to a knock on my door, and then the turn of the handle and it's Christian again. He crouches down and puts his hand on my forehead.

'Yeah, yeah, thought so.' He comes back into the room with his golden tray and puts it down on the floor. He sits me up and pours frothing, herby tea from a small brass teapot.

'Hot, hot,' he cautions and makes little blowing noises like a mother to a child.

It's all I can do not to cry.

'Yeah, yeah, you're not, you know, being yourself these days,' he says. I sniff and sip.

'Your root chakra asks only one thing. Do I belong here?' he says.

'I don't know if I do, Christian.'

It becomes a lullaby, the hot tea, the light of

Christian's candle on the golden tray and his long fingers moving in the air. He tells me about dreams and déjà vu; he tells me about reading tea leaves and palms, about sound baths and the mysteries of indigo, and so he goes on until he's covering me over with another blanket and placing his hand on my head.

Christian comes down the next day and the day after. I feel better on the third day and his stream of consciousness, his constant chatter, begins to grate.

'I'm going to see my sister,' I say when he lets himself in that evening. I've got my coat on and a duffle bag on my shoulder.

'Oh, oh, yeah, I mean, yeah. I'll walk you to the bus stop, you know—'

'No, it's only on Sandford Road . . .'

He opens the front door for me, waves when I turn. I float back in the small hours as it's getting light, stoned to beggary, and sleep all the next day. I don't see Christian for weeks afterwards. He's gone home to Staffordshire for grounding and a financial top-up. Weeks spill into months and Symanski eventually puts all his things into a cardboard box and lets his room to a middle-aged boozer called Leo.

I'm in The Fighting Cocks in Moseley Village when I hear the news. I swallow hard, push through the crowd to the back door and lean against the wall. I'm stoned as fuck as usual, and it takes ages to process that Christian is dead. Hanged himself in his mother's house. Left a note telling her she shouldn't worry. Death is just a temporary thing. He'd be back.

I roll myself a spectacular, five-Rizla spliff and suck on it all the way home. I sit on my cushions with shaking hands. I hear a moth against the window, but when I turn it stops suddenly, its fat brown belly hard on the glass. I wonder for a moment if it's Christian maybe, saying goodbye. And then I remember the scriptures that tell me that it can't be, that he's dead without hearing my thanks, a kind soul, gone for good.

22

For two years, my days don't change. I follow a pattern of afternoon waking, getting stoned, listening to music, signing on in Moseley Village, cashing my giro, feeling momentarily flush, buying weed, listening to bands in The Fighting Cocks, talking. There are riots all over England. Sus laws are putting innocent black people behind bars. Police brutality is the norm. We are angry. We are impotent.

I meet Pablo through a sort of boyfriend, Skip. It's summer and the heat has risen to Skip's attic flat in Handsworth. All the windows are open and everywhere, up the road and down, people are playing roots and rockers with the occasional slice of lovers' rock for flavour.

We're playing draughts on a piece of painted plywood, skipping the counters over the board, smoking and laughing. The door opens and a white man steps inside followed by a black woman who is dressed in African robes. She's easily six foot tall.

'Yo, yo, yo!' shouts Skip and, as he stands on

unsteady legs, the board tips over and the game is done.

They all embrace, hard. 'Come, come,' says Skip, 'sit, man! Long time.'

'True,' says Pablo and I expect him to be one of those white men who speak patois, all the right words, all the right music, with the wrong accent. But Pablo just sits there in a Geography teacher's corduroy jacket. He takes out an old man's pipe, fills it with weed and talks like a newsreader, every word clear, good English, deep and strong.

'When you come back?' says Skip.

'About four weeks ago,' he says and passes me the pipe with a nod.

'Seen, seen. Mandy, man, this is Madura, my cousin. And this my spar, Pablo. We meet in Winson Green, share a cell seven months.'

'Nine, I think,' says Pablo, 'if you count the extra weeks.'

They start laughing, and then the conversation turns to the riots and the state of the country. Pablo's political knowledge is startling.

After a long speech that takes in the slave trade, communism, reparation and Orientalism, he takes a pause and then begins again. 'It's a question of ownership and agency,' he says, but Madura cuts him off.

She speaks like a man, unapologetic, confident, the light glinting off her two gold teeth, her bangles clinking together every time she raises her hand.

'You think Thatcher want to spend money on us, even money to lock us up? She don't want us in prison! She want us out of the country, off the face of the earth. Mek dem go home! Yes! We finish with them now the country is on its feet, we finish with the black man. You think Thatcher want slavery done?'

She takes the pipe and we are all quiet while she thinks.

I don't have the words for what I feel, the hurt of my people, the anger and confusion. I fall into the role of seeker of truth and ask questions – why, how, when.

Red-eyed Pablo nods, fills the pipe, passes the pipe, and the sun sets. Eventually they get up to leave. I see Skip take Pablo to one side.

'You good?' he asks him. He's inches from his face, scanning it for something.

Pablo nods.

'Me ask you if you is good, Pablo,' Skip says again.

'Really, I am. Yes,' says Pablo. 'Clean.'

Madura kisses me and calls me sister. 'One love,' she says and then they're gone.

A few months later I see Pablo coming out of the chemist in Moseley Village. He looks different, tired maybe.

'Ah,' he says, 'I met you at Skip's, right? How is he?'

'Good, I think, I don't see him any more. How is . . .?'

'Madura? She's touring, speaking. She's opened the Black Women's Collective. It takes up all her time, I'm afraid.' We're walking downhill towards the park.

'We met when we were children. I'm Jamaican.'

I turn to take a better look. White people from Jamaica aren't unusual but the voice is. He smiles. 'My father sent me to England to be educated. Boarding school, Oxford, that sort of thing. Trying to wash out the black blood, I think.'

We sit on concrete steps by the outdoor theatre where a girl strums a guitar. I light a spliff and pass it to him.

The singing girl isn't very good. Pablo starts mid-sentence.

'That's what happened in Kashmir, you learn you need very little, actually. Took me three years to learn that. Came home. We all come home.'

He carries on and I realize he thinks he's told

me the first half of the story: something about losing everything and living off his wits, and his father refusing to send him the money to come home.

'I learned to speak fluent Kashmiri. It does me no good here.'

He starts speaking in a language which sounds beautiful and strange on his tongue.

'It's a story about a fish and a bridge. I forget the rest.'

As it grows darker, friends arrive from the village, singers and poets, artists, dossers, three of the 'we only wear red' brigade, one Hare Krishna, a white Rasta. I smoke some excellent Lebanese black with a guy who makes me laugh, and we dribble home to my flat for a few days until his stash of weed is used up.

I see Pablo from time to time in pubs, at gigs, at parties, slipping into Moseley life and growing shabby. He loses weight and his teacher's wardrobe. He shaves his head badly and the cuts get infected.

One night in The Fighting Cocks, I see he's lost some teeth and his face is bruised under the dirt. I feel a lump of sorrow grow in my chest for the man I met on a summer's night, when I listened to a queen and learned something new about the world. I feel a lump of sorrow in my throat for Christian and for the mother who found him. I can't seem to breathe.

'You wouldn't happen to have a few pounds, would you?' he asks.

'Sorry, Pablo, no, I don't. I'll buy you a drink,' I say.

'Can I have the money instead?'

It's such a bald and desperate ask, I give him some coins in spite of myself and he shuffles away. I see him sidle up to someone else, who shakes his head. And again.

And again, until he's lost in the crowd.

'Junked-up chancer,' says my friend.

I'm walking down Strensham Hill to a lock-in at The Black Eagle. I'd rather not, but I've been swept along somehow. These are not my friends, just people I smoke with, drink with. I feel like if I go to The Black Eagle, something bad might happen. I'm not even stoned. I'm anxious. I'm tired.

We are waiting to cross over the road when I see Pablo shuffling along. He's looking for cigarettes on the pavement. I feel something slip inside. He walks past me without looking up and I watch him go. He walks down Park Road and up to the door of a big, old house everyone knows as a squat and pushes it open. I follow.

'See you there later!' I shout to my non-friends.

The door opens easily and I walk inside. I walk through, no one stops me. In the kitchen, there's an old sofa with its guts ripped out and on that sofa is Pablo, picking the scab on his face.

'Pablo, you OK?' I say. He doesn't look up.

'No,' he says. 'She's really sick.'

'Who?'

He gets up and goes into a small room at the very back of the house. It's darker still. The air is thick with something decaying. There, lying on a mattress under a blanket, is a woman with dirty, sour-cream hair. She's skinnier and her skin is a type of yellow-green, but she's still Faye.

I kneel down and take her hand because I can see she doesn't recognize me.

'Faye, Faye, remember me? It's Mandy. Garretts Green College. Typing.'

'Mandy,' she says, but her eyes are closed.

'Mandy,' I repeat. 'You were going to America. Remember?'

'Mandy,' she says. Her eyes flicker open. 'Yeah. Nice handwriting.'

'Yes, me.'

Then she turns back to the wall and pulls the blanket over her face.

'What's wrong with her?' I ask Pablo.

'I'm taking her to the doctor tomorrow,' he says quickly.

'I said what's fucking wrong with her?'

'It's cold. Pretty difficult keeping this room warm in actual fact.'

I stand up. I back away bit by bit, looking at the narrow body under the blanket, the filth, the girl gone, the thing in her place. Pablo follows me out of the room.

'Have you got a fiver?' he asks and I shake my head.

'Fuck off.'

On the way home there are noises behind hedges and shadows on the pavement. Everything is very loud: the wind in the trees, cars driving past. I am petrified.

By the time I open the door to my flat I'm breathing so hard my chest hurts. There's a sort of loud humming, a buzzing like there's a fly trying to escape, and I wonder if it's Christian.

I open the curtains and throw the blankets off the bed because, if I can't find the fly, I can't help him come back as a human.

I go back into the street, but it's too dark for flies. A man walks past on the other side of the road. I can hear his thoughts. He's thinking about selfish people who won't give money to dying friends, so I run back inside and draw the curtains.

All I can do is wait for morning. My legs are shaking. I search my pockets for a spliff and find half an inch, barely enough to last ten minutes, let alone a whole night.

Dawn comes slowly. It's the longest night of my life. At six o'clock I put my coat on and start walking. I walk through the city centre, deserted and frightening. I walk and walk, crying all the time. I want my mom.

I find her in the maternity ward of Dudley Road Hospital, finishing her shift.

'Mandy, love,' she says and holds my hand, takes me wordlessly to a quiet room.

'I think I'm going mad, Mom.'

She bundles me into her arms and I sob on her shoulder.

'You're not going mad, love. Honestly, you're not.'

'I think I am.'

'Well, if you are, so am I. We'll be mad together.'

She sits me down on one of the chairs and wipes my face with a corner of her cardigan.

'Can you talk to me about something, Mom? Anything.'

'Well, we had this little baby born about half an hour ago. Chinese. You should have seen his hair. He was overdue, must have spent those two weeks growing a toupee.'

On and on and on she goes, about the babies and the mothers and what she'll make for dinner. And why don't I come home for a rest and shall we push the boat out and get a taxi, or do I feel like walking?

I lie in all my clothes in my childhood bed under the narrow window by the door. Mom comes in and strokes my forehead until my legs stop moving and I fall asleep.

When I come down in the morning, Dad is making corn porridge.

'Hungry?' he says and I shake my head and sit at the table.

'Course you is. When last you eat? Eat this.'

The plate is in front of me, hot and fragrant. He puts a spoon on the table and sits opposite me. If he's nice, I might cry.

'You want evaporated milk? Cool it down?'

I hold the spoon but can do nothing with it.

'What?' he says.

'I don't feel well,' I say. 'I think I'm going to die.'

He kisses his teeth. 'You think you is the only

one?' But I hear something in his voice, some piece of worry, some piece of love, and the tears spill.

'Wait,' he says and takes the plate. He brings it back with evaporated milk swirled into the porridge. 'That will cool it down. Eat it.'

I dip the spoon in, take half a mouthful, swallow it down. He watches.

'Good,' he says.

23

'And why do you want the job as Committals Clerk with the Office of the Chief Crown Prosecutor, Miss O'Loughlin?'

I'm wearing a new dress and Mom has given me one of her Jehovah's Witness coats to wear.

'I think it would be really interesting,' I say because this is the fifth interview this week, and the truth is that I'll do anything to fill my days and weary me enough at night to let me sleep.

The woman reads my certificates again and passes me a pad and a pencil for a shorthand test. She picks up a piece of paper and starts reading.

'Regina vs Benjamin Southall. On the second day of June in the City of Birmingham . . .'

It's easy but, better than that, it's interesting. It's a burglary and assaulting a police officer. I type it up eagerly and give it back to her in a few moments. When she raises her eyebrows, I know I've got the job.

My days are full of dictation by prosecution solicitors, who did what to whom and why and what's the evidence. The days are full but, without a spliff, without a drink, the nights are everlasting.

Sometimes I'm still awake as the sky turns from black to grey and can only sleep as it's getting light, and I feel safe again.

One day, I'm taking dictation from Mr Amway, senior prosecutor. He has a soft voice, slight touch of West Country.

'. . . under the Offences Against the Person Act 1861 this offence can only be made out if . . .' I yawn. He notices.

'Late night?' he says. He's a stout man in a stripy shirt with a white collar and spectacles. I know he thinks I'm out at parties and clubs with a boyfriend, dancing the night away, up at all hours.

'Couldn't sleep,' I say. 'Sorry.'

He resumes. '. . . and this offence can only be made out if we can prove intention or recklessness. . .' I yawn again.

'Worry or excitement?' he asks.

'Sorry?'

'Not sleeping. Worry or excitement?'

'Worry.'

'Ah. I see,' he says.

He gets up and stands by the big windows that overlook the city centre. 'What you need is a good book. That's what I do. Have a couple by the bed for the "four-o'clock-in-the-mornings" as I call them. You know, swirling thoughts. Pick up a book and you'll forget all about your troubles.'

The four-o'clock-in-the-mornings have lasted for months and I am desperate.

'What would you suggest?' I say. 'Give me your top ten books.'

'Oh,' he says, surprised. 'Well, let me see.'

He sits back down on his leather chair. He screws up his eyes and says nothing for a few minutes. Then he points at my notepad.

'Take this down.'

Fair Stood the Wind for France by H. E. Bates

Three Men in a Boat by Jerome K. Jerome

The Siege of Krishnapur by J. G. Farrell

The Riddle of the Sands by Erskine Childers

Madame Bovary by Gustave Flaubert

Thérèse Raquin by Émile Zola

Les Misérables by Victor Hugo

The Red Badge of Courage by Stephen Crane

Le Grand Meaulnes by Alain-Fournier

The Red and the Black by Stendhal

'That should keep you going,' he says.

After work, I hurry into the biggest bookshop I know. I buy Mr Amway's selection, all of them. I put them in a little pile next to the bed. I have never heard of a single author of a single title, so I start at the top with *Le Grand Meaulnes*. It's a story about a boy in France. I fall asleep to the sound of his clogs on the cobbles of Sologne.

Émile Zola describes near-madness in *Thérèse Raquin*, 'falling into a dark, cold hole'. I can hardly turn the page for wondering what will happen to the two murderers, but between the tension and the grief, he tells me that I'm not alone.

Gustave Flaubert makes me cry for Emma Bovary, the ordinary woman looking for that one thing more, her boredom, her discontent, not fitting in the right place and then her only way out. I read the same passage again and again.

'You forget everything. The hours slip by. You travel in your chair through centuries you seem to see before you, your thoughts are caught up in the story . . . you enter into characters, so that it seems as if it were your own heart beating beneath their costumes.'

They last only a few weeks, those ten books. Soon, I'm back in the bookshop.

I go on and on like this, week after week, month after month. If I wake, I turn on the light and reach down. I'm in Nepal, I'm in Brighton, I'm in Vienna. I'm a nurse, I'm a thief, I'm a soldier.

I start to think I might not die. I might find a way to live through books and other people's lives. I might have children. I might grow up. I think of all the books in the bookshop in town, thousands of them, millions. It would be years before I got through them all and there's new ones every week. I'd be an old lady before I got to the end.

I turn the page and keep reading. I'm going to live.

First published in Great Britain in 2022 by Tinder Press
An imprint of HEADLINE PUBLISHING GROUP

This Quick Reads edition published in 2024 by Tinder Press
An imprint of HEADLINE PUBLISHING GROUP

1

Cataloguing in Publication Data is available from the British Library

ISBN 978 1 0354 1368 3

Designed and typeset by EM&EN
Printed and bound in Great Britain by Clays Ltd, Elcograf S.p.A.

Headline's policy is to use papers that are natural, renewable and recyclable
products and made from wood grown in well-managed forests and other
controlled sources. The logging and manufacturing processes are expected
to conform to the environmental regulations of the country of origin.

HEADLINE PUBLISHING GROUP
An Hachette UK Company
Carmelite House
50 Victoria Embankment
London EC4Y 0DZ

www.tinderpress.co.uk
www.headline.co.uk
www.hachette.co.uk

About Quick Reads

"Reading is such an important building block for success"
~ Jojo Moyes

Quick Reads are short books written
by best-selling authors.

Did you enjoy this Quick Read?

Tell us what you thought by filling in
our short survey. Scan the **QR code**
to go directly to the survey or
visit **bit.ly/QR2024**

Thanks to Penguin Random House and Hachette and to all
our publishing partners for their ongoing support.

A special thank you to Jojo Moyes for her generous donation in
2020–2022 which helped to build the future of Quick Reads.

Quick Reads is delivered by The Reading Agency, a UK charity
with a mission to get people fired up about reading, because
everything changes when you read.

www.readingagency.org.uk   @readingagency   #QuickReads

The Reading Agency Ltd. Registered number: 3904882 (England & Wales)
Registered charity number: 1085443 (England & Wales)
Registered Office: 24 Bedford Row, London, WC1R 4EH
The Reading Agency is supported using public funding by
Arts Council England.

Supported using public funding by
**ARTS COUNCIL
ENGLAND**

Find your next Quick Read...

For 2024 we have selected 6 popular
Quick Reads for you to enjoy!

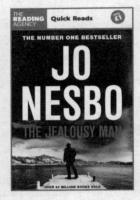

Quick Reads are available to buy in paperback or ebook and to borrow from your local library. For a complete list of titles and more information on the authors and their books visit **www.readingagency.org.uk/quickreads**

Continue your reading journey with The Reading Agency:

Reading Ahead

Challenge yourself to complete six reads by taking part in **Reading Ahead** at your local library, college or workplace: **readingahead.org.uk**

Reading
Groups
for Everyone

Join **Reading Groups for Everyone** to find a reading group and discover new books: **readinggroups.org.uk**

World Book Night

Celebrate reading on **World Book Night** every year on 23 April: **worldbooknight.org**

Summer Reading Challenge

Read with your family as part of the **Summer Reading Challenge: summerreadingchallenge.org.uk**

For more information on our work and the power of reading please visit our website: **readingagency.org.uk**

More from Quick Reads

If you enjoyed the 2024 Quick Reads
please explore our 6 titles from 2023.

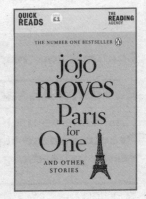

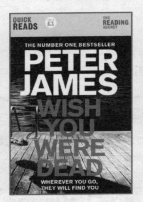

For a complete list of titles and more information
on the authors and their books visit:
www.readingagency.org.uk/quickreads